TOMIE dePAOLA

Christmas Remembered

G. P. PUTNAM'S SONS

I have tried to be as honest as I could with everything in this book, including the holiday eating and drinking in my family, but if you want to read this to your children, grandchildren, or your classes, feel free to "edit" or omit the drinking spots.

Coming from an Irish-Italian family, we always had "spirits" in our hearts, our life, and in our glasses.

As Hilaire Belloc said, "Wherever the Catholic sun doth shine, There's always laughter and good red wine. At least I've always found it so. *Benedicamus Domino!*"

G. P. PUTNAM'S SONS
A division of Penguin Young Readers Group.
Published by The Penguin Group.
Penguin Group (USA) Inc., 375 Hudson Street, New York, NY 10014, U.S.A.
Penguin Group (Canada), 90 Eglinton Avenue East, Suite 700, Toronto, Ontario, Canada M4P 2Y3
(a division of Pearson Penguin Canada Inc.).
Penguin Books Ltd, 80 Strand, London WC2R 0RL, England.
Penguin Ireland, 25 St. Stephen's Green, Dublin 2, Ireland (a division of Penguin Books Ltd.).
Penguin Group (Australia), 250 Camberwell Road, Camberwell, Victoria 3124, Australia
(a division of Pearson Australia Group Pty Ltd).
Penguin Books India Pvt Ltd, 11 Community Centre, Panchsheel Park, New Delhi - 110 017, India.
Penguin Group (NZ), Cnr Airborne and Rosedale Roads, Albany, Auckland 1310, New Zealand
(a division of Pearson New Zealand Ltd).
Penguin Books (South Africa) (Pty) Ltd, 24 Sturdee Avenue, Rosebank, Johannesburg 2196, South Africa.
Penguin Books Ltd, Registered Offices: 80 Strand, London WC2R 0RL, England.

Published simultaneously in Canada. Manufactured in China by South China Printing Co. Ltd.
Design by Cecilia Yung and Gina DiMassi. Text set in Centaur bold.
Library of Congress Cataloging-in-Publication Data
De Paola, Tomie.   Christmas remembered / Tomie dePaola.   p. cm.   1. De Paola, Tomie—Homes and haunts
2. Authors, American—20th century—Biography 3. Illustrators—United States—Biography 4. Christmas
I. Title.   PS3554.E11474Z46 2006   813'.54—dc22   2005032658
ISBN 0-399-24622-3
1 3 5 7 9 10 8 6 4 2
First Impression

For everyone I've ever spent Christmas with—
especially Bob Hechtel,
who has decorated more trees,
with more lights, more ornaments,
and more paper roses,
than Santa Claus himself.

Contents

Preface

IT'S NO SECRET THAT CHRISTMAS IS MY FAVORITE TIME OF THE YEAR. It has been ever since I can remember. *Why* it is my favorite time changes with each Christmas. Some have been superb. Some magical. Some transcendent—and mystical. And some have been awful! But as I enter my seventy-plus years of Christmases, I can look back on almost all of them with affection and an occasional boisterous chuckle.

Now, I do not remember my first Christmas. I have a good memory, but not that good. I can't remember the next one or the one after that either. But I have glimpses of them because in the fall of 1935, my father got an eight-millimeter Kodak movie camera and proceeded to document family events. Only my first Christmas in 1934, when I was three and a half months old, remains shrouded in mystery.

I still have movies of my older brother, Joe Jr. (or Buddy, as we called the family's first-born son), when he was five and I was a little over a year old. It is Christmas morning and he is sitting at his brand-new desk, built by my father and our family friend Tony Nesci. Buddy is wearing an art deco–patterned flannel robe (that I would kill for today). He moves some lead soldiers across the wood surface of the desktop. He opens and closes one of several Big Little Books sitting off to the right. Then he puts away his soldiers and his books and closes the desktop.

I'm in a high chair nearby, smiling and waving—more or less—at the camera with no presents in sight. Later in the film, I'm sitting in a toy airplane on the front porch, bundled up in a snowsuit, looking like a caterpillar wrapped in a cocoon waiting for spring. I'm sure the plane was one of the presents Santa brought Buddy several years earlier when he was the one-and-only dePaola heir. I still wonder what Santa brought me that Christmas.

So, alas, even with these brief moments, Christmas of 1934, 1935 and 1936 will always be buried deep in my subconscious. But I have more than enough memories to make up for those years. They are all as true as I can remember and, I hope, filled with the love I feel for all the family and friends with whom I have shared Christmases—past, present and ones to come.

Now I share some of them with you.

The Miraculous Christmas Fireplace

In 1937, when I was a little over three years old, my mother and father, Buddy and I lived in an apartment on Columbus Avenue in Meriden, Connecticut. My sister Maureen wouldn't be born until 1940, and the youngest, Judie, came along three years after that.

A few days before Christmas Eve, a fireplace miraculously appeared in our small living/dining room. It stood against the wall where, the day before, a china cupboard had stood. I can still see the red brick and my mother, the indomitable Flossie, unrolling a long piece of cotton batting from its blue paper wrapping and putting it across the mantel of the newcomer fireplace. She then carefully placed some glittery reindeer and tiny cardboard houses and buildings along the cotton. The houses and buildings had colored paper windows, and when a string of colored Christmas lights was inserted into the backs of the tiny structures, everything glowed. It was the Christmas Village. I was still too young to help sprinkle the mica snow that came in a box over the houses and the cotton snow. But I clearly remember the glowing village on the mantel of the red brick fireplace and the radiating flicker of the "burning logs" that reflected firelight into the room. I'm sure we had a Christmas tree, but I don't remember it.

It is no wonder that Christmas became my favorite holiday. It was a time of miracles—fireplaces appearing so Santa could visit, Flossie's famous Christmas Village that all the neighbors came to see, and a glittering rotating "fire" in the fireplace that never seemed to consume the logs, although I can still remember the smell of "burning."

I didn't find out about the "miraculous fireplace" until a few years later, when we moved into our new house and we had a *real* fireplace. I went down into the basement to snoop around. There, tucked away in a corner, its back facing the room, was the artificial fireplace. The brick was crepe paper. The "fire" was a gizmo that plugged in and rotated around a red lightbulb hidden under the plaster of Paris logs. The blazing fire was found out!

Well, never mind, I thought. *Santa would come down our real chimney and out through our real fireplace to bring us bigger and better toys!*

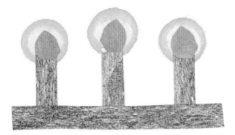

A Fairmount Avenue Christmas

Christmas traditions were big at our house—the perfect Christmas tree, red-and-white stockings embroidered with our names hanging on the stairway just below the banister, the Christmas Village, decorations and lights inside and out, Flossie's famous eggnog, and family and friends coming to celebrate in our magical "Christmas House."

For our first Christmas on Fairmount Avenue, my mother gave the place of honor on the fireplace mantel to a Nativity scene. We called it our "manger scene." The Christmas Village still remained a favorite. It was set up on the built-in buffet in the corner of the dining room and eventually my mother added ice-skating figures performing on a mirror "lake" and skiers schussing down a cotton-batting hill. It was always sprinkled with mica snow.

Other traditions would come to stay—blue electric candles in all the windows, a spotlit wreath or "spray" on the front door, blue lights on the bushes in the front yard. (Eventually the brass angel chimes I bought in Greenwich Village when I went to Pratt Institute in Brooklyn would ring throughout the living room.) And the Christmas tablecloth for people to sign with their Christmas greetings would be pulled out year after year—the stains of countless eggnogs attesting to this.

Every year my father, Joe, Buddy and I went looking for the perfect tree. It always seemed as if everyone in Meriden was out looking too. It took a couple of hours, but once we found the right tree, my father tied it to the roof of the car and we drove home.

My father would cut a little bit off the bottom of the trunk and set it in a pail of water. It stood on the side porch until we were ready for it. Then he would take it inside, put it in a tree stand and let it "relax" overnight.

Decorating the tree a few days before Christmas was a big event. My father put the strings of lights on first, then watched while my mother, Buddy and I carefully decorated the tree. All but the tinfoil icicles. "Okay," he would say, "time to put on the icicles." He would give each of us a small handful. Being the "artistic" one, I would slowly drape one strand at a time on the branches so as not to obscure the best ornaments and the multicolored lights that dotted the tree.

Buddy would cave in first. "Here," he'd say to me, "you do mine."

Gladly, I would think to myself.

Then it would happen. My father would grab a handful of icicles and hurl them at the tree like some crazy man set out to destroy our "fabulous Christmas tree that all the neighbors would come and see," my mother would say, almost in tears. Shouts of "Dad, you are ruining our tree!" from me. Buddy would just stand and watch, a big grin on his face.

Finally, icicles gone, we would calm down. Flossie and Joe would make each other a drink and give Buddy and me Cokes, which in my

day were something special, especially if they had ice cubes in them, frozen in one of the two trays in our monitor-top refrigerator.

My mother would turn out all the lights in the living room and turn on the blue electric candles in the windows and the star on the top of the stable in the manger scene. Next, she would turn on the Christmas Village.

With a big intake of breath, we kids could hardly stand it.

"Okay, boys," my father would say. "Here we go!"

He'd flip the switch and the tree would light up. So, who cared if those icicles were all clumped up on certain parts of the tree? To us it was always beautiful.

We stood there, just our family. It was sheer magic.

A Postwar Christmas

I WAS ELEVEN IN THE FALL OF 1945. The Second World War had ended in Europe in May and the Pacific in August. The coming Christmas promised to be "just like they used to be."

So much had been rationed during the four years of the war. Christmas tree lights hadn't been available. Sugar was one of the foods rationed, so candy canes, ribbon candy and hard candy were scarce. And so many regulations. Because of air raid warnings, no decorations or lights had been allowed in the downtown shopping area. Some people, my father included, had put colored electric candles in the windows and colored lights on the bushes outside. But, because of blackout restrictions, they were allowed to be on for only a few hours every night.

Christmas newspaper ads started early that fall. All the hardware stores as well as Kresge's, Woolworth's and W. T. Grant's advertised: "Christmas lights are back!" "Once again, an old-fashioned Christmas." "Get your Christmas lights now. Don't wait and be disappointed!"

My father wasted no time in buying all-new strings and extra bulbs. "We'll have a tree just like we used to have before Hitler and Tojo!" he declared. I knew what this meant—new icicles too! During the war, when we took down the tree, we had to remove the tinfoil icicles carefully, smooth them out and put them back in their boxes.

Flossie wanted to "renovate" the manger scene to celebrate the end of the war. We'd get new manger scene figures, "bigger ones," she said. So, she bought a Mary, Joseph and the Baby Jesus (all marked "Made in Italy") and added new ones (three shepherds, the Three Kings, three camels, an ox, a donkey, some sheep, a palm tree and two angels, make-believe hay for the manger, and a flying angel holding a banner that read "Gloria in Excelsis Deo"). There was no stopping Flossie! Our manger scene would rival the big one at St. Joseph's.

By Christmas Eve, the house was decorated and lights were on inside and out. All of our presents were wrapped and stacked under the "perfect Christmas tree."

Maureen and Judie got into their new nightgowns, bathrobes and slippers (we always got new pajamas or nightgowns, bathrobes and slippers for Christmas, even during the war) and came downstairs.

We did the ritual of turning off the lights inside the house, then lighting the electric candles in the windows, the Christmas Village, the manger scene, and then—the tree, with more clumps of icicles than ever.

We kids were allowed to open one present each. The rest would

have to wait until Christmas morning, along with all the stuff from Santa Claus.

The girls went to bed, and for the first time I was allowed to stay up for the "open house" that Flossie and Joe had every Christmas Eve. All the neighbors came, as well as my parents' friends and family from all over Meriden and Wallingford. The drinks were served in the half of the basement my father had fixed up with booths and a genuine bar. "Just like a real nightclub, Floss and Joe," everyone said. The "nightclub" was really hopping on this first Christmas Eve since the war.

At midnight, Flossie had that look in her eye. Buddy had already packed it in. He certainly wasn't a "party animal" the way I seemed to be. He was fifteen and already upstairs asleep.

"Tomie," my mother said quietly, "why don't you go up to bed. The girls will be up early and you can help them open their presents and sort out Santa's gifts. Say good night to everyone."

I knew no argument would work and, if truth be told, I was tired.

I went up, and the next thing I knew, Maureen was whispering in my ear, wanting to go and see what Santa brought. Judie was still pretty young, so she was "following the leader."

I put on my new bathrobe and we went downstairs. My mother was already there and the Christmas tree was lit. "Merry Christmas," she said. "And look what Santa brought." Around the tree and flowing out into the living room were toys, dolls, games, so much stuff.

"But first," my mother said, "come see Baby Jesus. He came last night too." She picked up Judie and I held up Maureen so they could see the figure of the Baby Jesus lying in the manger on the mantel.

Then all of our attention turned to the presents under the tree.

I found my pile from "Santa." One present after another was art supplies just for me—an oil paint set, a watercolor set, an easel, pastels, pads of drawing and watercolor paper, colored pencils and books on how to draw things. I was speechless! I looked at each one over and over again.

My father and Buddy came in and I started showing them my art supplies. "Look!" I cried.

"Don't forget your other presents, Tomie," my mother said. More art supplies—a clay set, a wood-burning set, a set so I could make plaster of Paris plaques and paint them, a metal-embossing set and an envelope with a gift certificate for Lamphier's Paint and Art Supply Store. Even Buddy had given me a pen set from Speedball with India ink and pen points so I could learn to be a cartoonist. What a Christmas!

I could hardly tear myself away to go to Christmas Mass. After Mass, we all went up to the altar to look at the almost life-sized manger scene. I looked right at the figure of the Baby Jesus. "Thank you," I whispered. All my prayers were answered. Since I was four, I had been saying that I was going to be an artist when I grew up. Everyone had believed me.

I couldn't wait to get home and try out those pencils, paints and pastels on all those pads of paper. I thought my box of sixty-four Crayola crayons was special. Wait until I told Mrs. Bowers, our art teacher, about all the supplies I had now!

I've never forgotten the feeling I had that Christmas morning. The memory of it comes back every time I get an art-supply catalog in the mail. I hope that everyone who celebrates Christmas has as good a memory as this one. It's lasting a lifetime!

The First Television Christmas

AFTER THE WAR, MY FATHER WORKED AS A SALESMAN for Eder Brothers liquor distributor. The company had contests to encourage the salesmen to sell, sell, sell. The month they had one to see who could distribute the most cases of Imperial Blended Whiskey, my father won.

The prize was $1,000 or a television set. I'm sure the money could have gone a long way in 1947. My father earned about $4,000 a year, but we had a car, we owned our own home and we always had food on the table. (My Irish grandparents owned a grocery store in Wallingford.) I took tap-dancing lessons and Flossie and Joe were always having parties at our house. So what did we know? Of course, my father chose the television set.

The first thing I did was to read all about television in the "Book of Knowledge" encyclopedias, which had a place of honor on a shelf in what had been our garage until it was renovated and became the "Knotty Pine Room"—that is, until the RCA technicians arrived to hook up "the second set in all of Meriden." (The other set was in the showroom of an appliance store downtown.) The "Knotty Pine Room" quickly became the "TV Room."

I remember coming home from junior high on Wednesday, December 3, to find a tall metal tower, complete with guy wires and spokes, sticking up on the roof of our house. Flossie was looking at it in tears.

"It's ruined our lovely house," Flossie complained. "The workmen kept adding and adding to it. It's fifty feet high! Just wait until your father gets home."

I thought it was exciting. I ran inside and went right to the "Knotty Pine Room," and there against the back wall was the new set, looking gargantuan, even though the screen was about the size of the fishbowl my goldfish, Cleopatra, lived in. (She had a fantail body about the size of a fifty-cent piece, and her tail was bigger than her body and floated languidly around like some exotic dancer's veil.)

The television technicians had been getting short shrift from Flossie. They turned to me, looking relieved. "Hey, kid, can we show you how to tune in the set?" They told me that the RCA set was the top of the line. The twelve-inch picture tube was the biggest available, and it had the new RCA "Golden Throat" sound system—"the finest tone system in RCA Victor history."

"And even though you're one hundred miles from New York, you can get two channels pretty good," they said. "Channel 4—NBC and Channel 5—Dumont." Channel 2 was iffy, because "CBS doesn't have programs on except for weekends," they said, switching to Channel 2. The screen looked like a blizzard scene from *Nanook of the North*. (That was why they called TV interference "snow"!)

I knew that the nearest broadcasts came all the way from New York City, one hundred miles away, because no television transmission towers existed between Meriden and the Empire State Building in New York. Unlike radio waves, which followed the curve of the Earth, television traveled in a straight line.

I listened, watched, tried, succeeded and was given the official title of "TV Tuner." They gave me the instruction book, packed up their tools, apologized to Flossie for ruining her beautiful house and left.

I immediately sat down and began to read. I always—and still do—read instruction books that come with appliances or gadgets, even though it can be daunting—and sometimes funny—when the instructions have been translated into English by someone in the country that made the equipment.

My father told us that on Friday night, Joe Louis, the Brown Bomber and Heavyweight Champion of the World, was going to fight Jersey Joe Walcott, live from Madison Square Garden, and it was going to be televised. Flossie and Joe immediately invited all their friends to come and watch the fight.

The only other place in Meriden to see the fight was at the appliance store. They had advertised in the two newspapers that they were giving out free tickets, but they had limited space.

Word got around fast that the dePaolas had a television. "But we don't know 'em." "They're Democrats!" "I understand she's Irish and he's *Eye-talian*."

But none of that mattered on the night of December 5. I was sitting on the floor next to the television, ready to tune in the fight. Our friends had settled in the folding chairs my father had set up in the

TV Room and were enjoying the food and drink they had brought when the doorbell rang.

My father opened the door and standing there were complete strangers laden with pizzas, Coca-Cola, beer, ice cream, brownies and doughnuts. They had come to watch the fight on our television. Flossie and Joe welcomed them and brought them out to the TV Room. Everyone crowded in, and I tuned in the fight.

We were all riveted to the screen, watching Joe Louis stalking Jersey Joe Walcott, who was walking backward around the ring for fifteen rounds. Joe Louis got knocked down twice, but there was no knockout. No one cared. Even though it was a split decision, Joe Louis kept his title. Everyone in the room cheered as the referee bellowed, "Joe Louis, Still Heavyweight Champeen of the Woild!"

I tell this story because the new television played a romantic part in my life that Christmas Eve. I was in eighth grade and I had an "older woman" for my girlfriend. Her name was Sheila Rosenthal and she was in ninth grade.

I had gone to Sheila's house for a Hanukah party on Saturday, December 13, and she was coming to our house for Christmas Eve. After the dreaded Calabrese Christmas Eve supper of the Seven Fishes (have you ever eaten scungilli?), we went out to the TV Room. We sat on the sofa like two lovebirds, holding hands and stealing a few quick chaste kisses, while we gazed at the screen broadcasting a black-and-white image of a fire burning in a hearth. The blazing Yule log with a "Holiday Greetings" banner above it and Christmas songs playing in the background filled the screen from five in the afternoon until about ten at night.

Needless to say, Sheila and I were thrilled with our first TV Christmas. Never mind that we could have moved into the living room, where the Christmas tree was lit and a real log blazed in full color in a real fireplace. It just didn't dawn on us.

A Candy Cane Christmas

In 1948 our neighbors the Nadiles—Gladys and Joe and their daughters Paulette, who was Buddy's age, and Sheila, who was a little younger than I was—moved to Linsley Avenue. They had bought a small candy store downtown on Hanover Street, right around the corner from the main bus stop. It was called the Kandy Kettle. There's nothing better than having friends who own a candy store, and whenever I took the bus home from downtown, I stopped in at the Kandy Kettle.

Often Mrs. Nadile was behind the counter of glass cases, which displayed the most delicious homemade candy in the world. Even though Mr. Nadile was a teacher at the high school, he had thrown himself into candy making with all the artistry and invention that Italian artists have been practicing for centuries.

The shelves were filled with hand-dipped chocolates with the little swirls on top indicating what kind of fillings were inside: chocolate-covered caramels, buttercrunch, raspberry crème and, the best, chocolate-covered cherries. (I didn't like the maple crème or almond crème at all.) Not only were there exotic items like gooey, nutty, chocolate-covered "Turtles," but also "Bark" made of three kinds of chocolate—dark, milk and white. They offered chocolate and penuche fudge for the less adventurous, and cellophane-wrapped lollipops of every flavor imaginable, including spearmint, root beer and butterscotch, filled shiny glass jars on the top of the counters. I mean we're talking the Tiffany's of candy stores right here in Meriden, Connecticut.

I was always full of questions for Mrs. Nadile, but what I wanted to know the most was how Mr. Nadile made his "molasses sponge" candy. It was hard candy, yet light as a feather, and made of pale yellow-tan "molassesy"-tasting foam that dissolved on my tongue with a chewy crackle.

Mrs. Nadile must have remembered, because one day in early December, Mr. Nadile invited me to spend a Saturday afternoon in the "kitchen," the workroom where they made the candy. They were going to be cooking a batch of molasses sponge.

The "kitchen" had an enormous metal table in the middle. Off to one side was another good-sized table with a marble top, a triple sink and, on the wall, a giant metal hook. Tucked off in its own corner was a squat gas stove where the sugar, corn syrup, water and any other ingredients were heated to lavalike temperatures and made into candy. The stove accommodated various sizes of metal rings that could be added or removed to hold the round copper candy kettles, dark with heat patina on the outside and gleaming on the inside. A big tub next to the stove held half a dozen tall wooden paddles used to stir the bubbling mass as it was cooking. Bottles of flavorings, colors and extracts stood on the shelves around the workroom.

"Okay, Tomie, put this on," Mr. Nadile said, handing me a white apron that looked just like the one Tom, my grandfather, wore in his meat and grocery store.

"We're going to be dealing with some very hot stuff, so be careful and stand out of the way. The candy is as hot as *lava!*" he told me. He lit the stove with a *whoosh*, moved a ring or two, and put one of the copper kettles on the fire.

He poured in the molasses and added sugar and a few other ingredients. The mixture began to bubble like a witch's cauldron. He stirred the bubbling mass and checked it with a candy thermometer. "Okay," Mr. Nadile announced. "It's ready." Mr. Nadile poured in a big cupful of baking soda. The dark "lava" suddenly foamed up like nothing I had seen before.

A man who was there to help had arranged four metal bars in a rectangle on the lightly greased large table. They would keep the lava-hot mixture from flowing off onto the floor until it cooled down.

Wearing heavy gloves, Mr. Nadile and his helper picked up the kettle by its round handles and poured the hot foaming mixture onto the table. Mrs. Nadile opened a valve, which started cold water running through pipes under the metal surface of the table. "Cold water cools the candy off quickly," she told me. "The table can be used as a 'cold table' or a 'hot table'—whatever we need."

The bubbly mass of foam settled down, pushing up against the metal bars on the "cold table." Gradually the blanket of yellow-tan molassesy-smelling foam stopped seething and looked pretty solid. Mr. Nadile moved one of the metal bars. The edge of the foam was nice and firm. It was amazing. The bottom was a smooth layer of "taffy"; the top was more irregular; the entire middle looked exactly like a sponge, a veritable irregular honeycomb of spaces—just waiting to melt on the tongue of its greatest admirer. Me! Now I knew all the secrets of molasses sponge candy.

Mr. Nadile picked up a large half-circle cutter called a "mezza-luna," or half-moon, held it with both hands, chopped off a piece and gave it to me to eat. I thought it was the best I had ever tasted.

I stayed until it was time to close. Mrs. Nadile gave me a bag of molasses sponge to take with me. "Tell Flossie to put it in an airtight tin. It melts if it's in moist air."

The Nadiles gave me a ride home. On the way, they asked me if I would like to help them in the store at Christmas. Sheila would be helping too.

"Sure," I said. "Maybe we can wear red caps and be 'Santa's Helpers' in the kitchen." We did, and I ended up with two important jobs. The first was "crooking" the candy canes. The second was "crimping" the ribbon candy.

The Kandy Kettle was famous for its handmade candy canes and ribbon candy. They sold every "mint" flavor imaginable in candy canes—peppermint (of course), wintergreen, double-mint, clove, cinnamon and my favorite, spearmint. They made the same flavors in ribbon candy, as well as cherry, lime, orange, root beer and peanut butter filled.

We made the canes first. Mr. Nadile boiled the mixture of sugar, corn syrup and water in the copper kettle, then he poured it on the table. He divided it into one large piece and a number of smaller pieces that would become the colored stripes. First Mr. Nadile put the

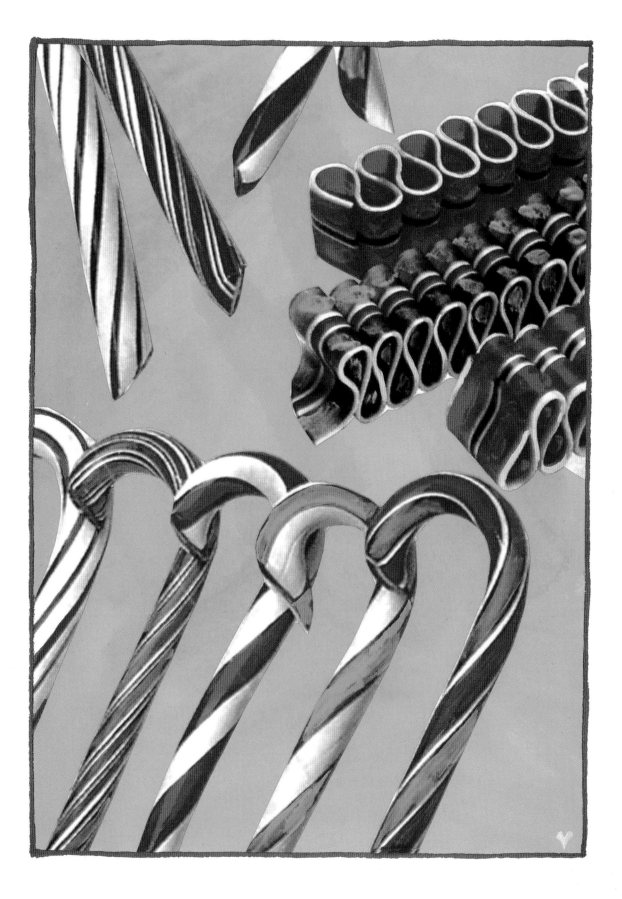

large piece on the wall hook and pulled it like taffy to add just enough air. When it turned white, he put it back on the table under a heat lamp to keep it pliable. Then he put the smaller pieces on the wall hook, adding flavoring and coloring for the stripes.

The colored taffy was pulled into long strips that were then put on the surface of the white block of candy. Mr. Nadile and his helper put on heavy heatproof gloves and began pulling the block of candy until it was the right size for candy canes. Then, they cut it into pieces with big shears. Next, they rolled the pieces so the stripes twirled up the cane. The bottom was rolled thinner than the top.

Now it was my turn to crook. I placed the canes along a heavy metal rod to keep them straight. I put a crook in each one before they cooled off. Then I moved them to a part of the table that was cold so they would harden. I had a good eye, so they were all "crooked" just right.

The ribbon candy started off the same way except it was pulled flat instead of rolled. A length would be cut off. I'd grab it with my left gloved hand and put the end into a contraption that put the first loose "crimp," or accordion fold, in it. I turned a handle with my right hand and when the length of candy came out, I'd gently push the ends to tighten the crimps. Just like the canes, I would move the ribbon candy to a cold part of the table to set.

Working at the Kandy Kettle was a great experience. I'll never forget the order we got a few days before Christmas. A man came in with an unusual request. His wife loved peppermint, and he wanted to surprise her with a candy cane as tall as she was.

Mr. Nadile was up for the task. The candy cane would be five foot three inches tall; it would have two thin stripes of green and a wider stripe of red against a white background; it would be peppermint flavored, of course. It was the last order we made before we closed for Christmas Eve.

When it was time to make the crook, Mr. Nadile let me do it. After it had cooled, the candy cane was lifted onto a wooden base, covered in clear cellophane and tied with ribbons.

We looked at our masterpiece and cheered. The customer was very impressed and pleased with our work.

It was time to close up shop and go home for Christmas Eve. Mr. Nadile gave everyone a little Christmas bonus and told us we all did a great job. "The next holiday is Valentine's Day, so rest up!"

"We'll see you later tonight at your folks' open house, Tomie," Mr. Nadile said as I left. "And thanks a lot. You're the best 'crooker and crimper' in Connecticut. Merry Christmas!"

The Christmas Sing

IF THERE WAS EVER A MAN IN MY SCHOOL LIFE WHO LOVED
CHRISTMAS, it was the high school vocal music teacher. The
Christmas Sing every December had become the event of the holiday
season in Meriden, thanks to Tony Parisi.

The Special Chorus began to learn songs early in October. Every
year, some "old favorites" would be pulled out of the fire and the lat-
est pop Christmas or winter holiday song would be rehearsed, as well
as classical pieces by the likes of Bach and Handel.

Songs were sung by young sopranos, fresh-faced tenors and baritones
and basses whose low voices didn't quite fit with their gawky bodies.

The middle of the program was the singing of traditional
Christmas carols such as "Joy to the World," "O Little Town of
Bethlehem" and "Silent Night."

Everyone was invited to join in and carol books, supplied by the
Metropolitan Life Insurance Company, were on every seat in the audi-
torium. The color cover was the same year after year—a nighttime
New England snow scene of a white wooden clapboard steeple church,
glowing windows and a tiny crowd of people streaming into the

26

church under a midnight blue sky. And wait! Is that a star of Bethlehem over the church?

Then the moment everyone was anticipating—the Special Chorus's performance of the musical version of "The Night Before Christmas," composed or commissioned by Fred Waring for his famous "Fred Waring and the Pennsylvanians." It was perfect for a good-sized chorus with a rich mixture of voices.

Before the chorus began singing, Tony Parisi would invite all former members of the Special Chorus home from college to join them onstage. A stream of young women and men filed down the aisles and took their places among the proper vocal group. (Four years later, I would be among them.) The piece went on for fifteen, twenty or twenty-five minutes with special solos interspersed throughout. It was always magical, and it always got a standing ovation.

I auditioned and was accepted for the Special Chorus in my sophomore year, the first year of high school in my day. Mr. Parisi liked my boy-soprano voice, and I began to hope that maybe I'd get to sing a solo in "The Night Before Christmas." I guess I was the closest thing to a prepubescent English choir boy in the whole of Meriden. In reality, I was short and I hadn't entered puberty yet—trust me—and I still had the clear bell tone that boy sopranos had.

Then it happened! Mr. Parisi asked me if I'd like to do a solo. He must have sensed that I thought I might get to sing one of the "Night Before Christmas" solos, because he explained, gently, that those solos only went to juniors and seniors. He told me that Miss Riley, who had been our junior high music teacher and was the organist at Holy Angels, where we went to church, had told him about me singing

"Under the Stars." He said he loved the song and that's what he wanted me to sing. Of course I said yes.

Then he surprised me with a different request. He must have seen the article on Christmas decorations in *The Meriden Record,* which wrote admiringly about the three life-sized medieval carolers I had painted and built (with my father's help) for our front lawn the year before.

The chorus always sang with an unadorned blue-black curtain behind them. Mr. Parisi hoped I could do some larger-than-life cutouts for a scenic decoration. He showed me a Christmas card of some Victorian English carolers with a "coach and four" that he thought would make a good backdrop.

I said I would, but I knew I would need help with the horses. I asked Miss Bishop, one of the art teachers, if Claire Gosselin could help. She could draw horses much better than I could. It took weeks of work, but when the curtain was opened and the audience saw the six- to eight-foot Victorian carolers clustered around a gaslit lamppost looking at Claire's wonderful "coach and four," complete with boxes and passengers, they burst out clapping.

My first Christmas Sing as a sophomore was sheer joy. I sang my solo, "Under the stars, one holy night, a blessed babe was born . . ." And during the next two years, I had those coveted solos in "The Night Before Christmas." "He spoke not a word, but went straight to his work . . ." in junior year and "The stump of a little ol' pipe he held tight in his teeth, and the smoke went around and around and around his head like a wreath . . ." in senior year.

Then, in my senior year, within weeks of the Christmas Sing, my voice changed—suddenly—without warning and all at once! I could still sing my "Night Before Christmas" solo as a high tenor, but Mr. Parisi had picked out another solo to show off my boy-soprano voice. Somehow "Once in Royal David's City" didn't sound quite the same as it should.

Crisis! But it was Flossie to the rescue. "Sing 'Rudolph the Red-nosed Reindeer,'" she suggested. I did, accompanied by my classmate, the beautiful Georgia Bradley, on the piano, and it was a great success.

By the way, I can still remember the words to "Under the Stars" if anyone is interested in a mid-baritone performance. I'm inexpensive—and available.

A Nana Fall-River Christmas

Besides the annual Christmas Sing, our Special Chorus went caroling. We'd pile on a bus in the early evening and head off. We'd visit the several nursing homes in Meriden, a "home for children"—not quite an "orphanage"—and the tuberculosis sanatorium called "Underhill." We sang outside the two hospitals and we would visit private homes if they called the high school and requested us. My mother always called. She'd gather the neighbors so we'd have a good-sized audience.

Tony Parisi and his wife, Tata, came to Flossie and Joe's "open house" every year. "Tony," Flossie said, "those Special Chorus kids do such a good job. Does anyone ever invite them in for some refreshments when they go caroling?"

"In all the years I've been doing this, no one has," Tony told my mother.

"Well, next year, come here last and I'll have hot chocolate and doughnuts for everyone," Flossie announced triumphantly. My mother was the ultimate parent cheerleader.

In no time at all, Christmas was coming again. We rehearsed for the annual Christmas Sing, and plans were afoot for the caroling that would take place on a weeknight right before high school closed for Christmas vacation.

A few nights before the caroling, my father told us that my Italian grandmother, whom I had called Nana Fall-River ever since I was a child, was going to stay a night or two on her way to the Bronx to spend Christmas with Aunt Kate, my father's sister.

Then Fate struck. Uncle Tony called to say that Aunt Kate wasn't feeling well and wouldn't be up to a visit from Nana. We shouldn't have been surprised. The same thing happened every year. Aunt Kate's health was always a bit tentative, especially around Christmas.

Nana Fall-River would spend Christmas with us. It wouldn't be too bad—not like the time she came for Easter and stripped all the coats from the front closet because her Easter bread wasn't rising fast enough. She decided the coats would keep the dough warmer.

My father had given Nana our old television set. She already had her favorite programs to watch during the day, mostly soap operas, and in the evening family was around, so she had lots of company.

The day after the Christmas Sing, Mr. Parisi told me that the Special Chorus wouldn't be able to come to our house for hot chocolate and doughnuts after all. A parent had called the principal to complain that only the Special Chorus went caroling, so they were opening it up to any kids who wanted to go.

But when Mr. Parisi saw me the next day, he said, "Tomie, you have quite a mother. She said she promised, and she doesn't care how many kids sign up."

A few days went by. Over two hundred kids signed up. That was five busloads.

But Flossie had it all planned. She enlisted the help of her "bridge club"—a group of women who got together twice a month to play cards and drink "Orange Blossoms." She called Knapp's Dairy to figure out how much milk she would need. She called the Vienna Bakery to special-order the doughnuts. "One a piece," she said. "And only one kind." For the hot chocolate, she borrowed large stockpots from the South Meriden House, a restaurant and bar nearby where she and my father were "regulars."

The night of the caroling went off without a hitch. The kids filed in through the front door and went directly to the kitchen for the hot chocolate and doughnuts. "It's a good thing we worked on the assembly line at New Departure during the war," Hazel Skinner quipped as she poured hot chocolate after hot chocolate into paper cups. "Only one doughnut," Polly Carroll, Flossie's best friend, repeated over and over again.

The line of kids filed out of the kitchen door, then through the TV Room, where Nana Fall-River was watching a program. As they passed my grandmother and went outside, they said, "Hello." "Merry Christmas." "Thank you, ma'am."

I don't think the whole event lasted more than an hour or so, it was so well organized. Of course we serenaded Flossie, the neighbors and the bridge club before the kids left. And, of course, the ladies broke out the "Orange Blossoms" when the buses had gone.

My father got home and went to say hello to Nana. "Josie (her nickname for "Giuseppe," my father's name in Italian), Firenze (Florence), she have so many people here. In they come, out they go, in they come," Nana complained.

"Didn't they say hello?" my father asked with hidden amusement.

"Yeh, sure, they say hello. Merry Christmas. Bye-bye. But," Nana said with indignation, "Firenze, she never introduce me to anyone!"

On Christmas Eve, Flossie and Joe had their "open house." Nana sat in the rocking chair by the blazing fireplace, watching everyone go down to the "nightclub and bar" in the basement.

Flossie mixed her "world-famous" eggnog and poured it into a cut-glass punch bowl. My father carried it into the dining room and put it on the dining room table with all the platters piled high with food. Soon the party was in full swing with kisses under the mistletoe, lots of laughter, and good food and drink. Everyone made a point of greeting my grandmother and introducing themselves. I suspect my father had something to do with that.

When most of the guests had gone into the kitchen or back down to the "nightclub," I sat with Nana, listening to her stories about Christmas in *her* country. (She had only been in America for forty-plus years.)

My father came in to check the fire and Nana grabbed his arm. "Josie," she whispered loudly. "What do you do? All these people—drinking, eating—so much. You worka so hard for your money. What do all these people do? Eat, eat, eat. Drink, drink, drink."

My father looked at her with a twinkle in his eye. "Oh, Ma, I'm not giving the food and drinks away. The people are buying them."

"Ah," my grandmother said, nodding.

The next wave of people that came into the room were greeted with "Have something nice to eat. Have another drink," from Nana.

A bit later, my father appeared.

"Hey, Josie," Nana whispered. "Come here!"

"Yeah, Ma, what is it?" my father asked.

"Business pretty good, huh?"

Nana Fall-River beamed.

A Pratt Christmas

In the fall of 1952, I headed off to Brooklyn, New York, to begin my dream of becoming an artist and to do it at Pratt Institute. This was the art school that my twin cousins, both professional photographers, had graduated from ten years earlier. They were my idols and mentors from the time I was a youngster. I wanted to be just like them—sophisticated, talented, kind, generous, glamorous, famous in their fields—you get the picture.

They were happy that I had been accepted at Pratt and were quick to give me advice. "Don't skimp on art supplies. Always buy the best," from Franny. "You'll like Mr. So-and-So at first because he's more like a high school teacher. But you'll find the other teachers more exciting and challenging enough, though they aren't necessarily friendly," from Fuffy. "Take advantage of New York. Go into Manhattan on Saturdays. Go to museums and galleries. It's all part of your art education," from Franny. "When you feel more comfortable with the big city, go to Greenwich Village," from Fuffy. "You'll love it!" they both told me.

I did as they suggested, and they were right. I *loved* Greenwich

Village. Talk about artsy and nonconformist. Everyone wore black (and this was in the fifties). Some of my classmates were "day students." They grew up in New York from the time they were babies, and they were great "tour guides." They knew all the best places, especially in the Village.

Time passed quickly from assignment to assignment. I was the busiest, and the most tired, I had ever been. But every Saturday I could, I hopped on the subway, only a ten-cent ride to Manhattan.

I "lived" in the Museum of Modern Art and the galleries on Fifty-seventh Street. I loved to window-shop along Fifth Avenue and check out Broadway and Times Square, much sleazier then than it is now, but so many lights! I certainly "wasn't in Kansas," as Dorothy said to Toto, or even Meriden for that matter.

Often on the way back to Brooklyn, I'd get off the subway at West Fourth Street and walk around the Village, rubbing shoulders with the "Beatniks" and "Bohemians."

At Thanksgiving I took the train home to Meriden to be with family and have our big Thursday dinner at Tom and Nana's house in Wallingford. When I returned to Grand Central on Sunday night, the station had been transformed. Huge green wreaths with red bows and green roping and more Christmas ornaments than you could imagine filled the waiting room. Carols were playing over loudspeakers. The Kodak sign, billed as "the biggest photograph in the United States," displayed a wintry night scene from Vermont or New Hampshire. New York had been very busy getting decorated for Christmas.

The buzz was on at Pratt. "Have you seen the animated windows at Lord & Taylor's?" "The ones at Wanamaker's are better." "I wonder how they'll do the tree at Rockefeller Center this year. Last year it was boring—all lights and huge red bows."

In those days, all the big department stores, most of them long gone now, tried to outdo one another with their decorations and window displays. Lord & Taylor's always got my vote, with Tiffany's coming in second.

I was so busy going into Manhattan with my small group of friends to see as much as we could that I almost forgot about going present shopping. It wouldn't be long before I would be heading back to Grand Central for the trip home. It was time to get serious.

I was away from home and on my own for the first time. I wanted to give everyone in the family perfect presents. I was realistic enough to know that I couldn't afford the fancy stores like Brooks Brothers, Dunhill's and Hammacher Schlemmer's, but it was a great excuse to prowl around, trying to look knowledgeable and rich, and maybe get some ideas. It was fun, but I was just fooling myself. I even checked out F.A.O. Schwarz, hoping to get a doll for Judie. But I ended up at Macy's (much cheaper).

Finally it was the Saturday before Christmas vacation and I wasn't finished shopping. I'd done some small paintings and matted them so they looked dressed-up and expensive, but I still had presents to get for Flossie and Joe, Buddy and Maureen. I would go to Manhattan and scour the Village, where prices were more reasonable.

First I went up to Rockefeller Center to watch the skaters and have one last look at the enormous Christmas tree towering over the ice-skating rink. As I left to go to the subway, I passed Dunhill's, which sold expensive lighters, pipes and stuff. There in the window was a

small box with a stylish cigarette holder and three filters to go with it "on sale." I'd get it for Buddy and tell him that the filters were good for his health. I knew it wasn't an appropriate present from my older brother. He smoked, but he was hardly the cigarette-holder type. But so be it. Maybe he'd "change."

I took the subway downtown and got off at West Fourth. I walked along the narrow Village streets and looked in windows full of possibilities. I found myself standing in front of one, when the smell of mulled wine wafted up from out of a basement shop called Jahn's. The sign read "Scandinavian Design." I went down the steps and into the store. A smiling young woman offered me a glass of warm *glögg*—mulled wine. I walked around sipping it slowly, enchanted by everything I saw.

I spotted a glass cocktail shaker with four glasses in sleek modern lines. It was practical and "arty," and my father would love it.

Now for Maureen. I combed through a display of hand-painted silk scarves and picked one out. Maureen would be the only girl in Lincoln Junior High with a silk scarf that looked as if I might have taken brushes full of paint and used the scarf as a canvas.

That left Flossie. I had noticed a tiny jewelry store right next to Jahn's. All the silver jewelry was handmade there. In the case, staring up at me, was a pin that looked like an abstract heart. Flossie wore it for years. I guess that was the very beginning of my love of the heart as a personal trademark.

So, who else in the family was sophisticated, talented, kind, generous and glamorous? *Someday I'll be famous in my field too!* I thought.

A Regina Laudis Christmas

DURING MY JUNIOR YEAR AT PRATT, a friend showed me a photo story about a small Benedictine monastery in Weston, Vermont. I was immediately intrigued. I knew very little about the Order of Saint Benedict, so I wrote the subprior, Father Bede, who promptly answered my letter and sent me a small booklet explaining the Benedictine life. I found out that art was held in high esteem and that I would not have to become a priest, but could be a "choir monk." Weston was attempting a return to a more "primitive" (or simple) way of life. More letters were written and received, so I went home to tell my parents that I wanted to enter a monastery in Weston, Vermont. Flossie and Joe weren't too pleased.

They must have talked to Father Moriarity, the pastor of our church, because he asked me if I would like to visit Regina Laudis, a Benedictine monastery of nuns in Bethlehem, Connecticut. He had "sponsored" Mother Benedict and Mother Mary Aline when they came from France to start this small community. I'm sure that he was secretly thinking that Reverend Mother Benedict, now the prioress of Regina Laudis, would "set me straight."

On the drive to Bethlehem, Father Moriarity explained that the monastery was cloistered. No one from the outside, except doctors, could go beyond the monastic gates and only with the permission of the Reverend Mother or the Bishop. Sisters called "extern" sisters handled any business conducted with the outside world.

When we arrived in the small, rural town, tucked into the Litchfield Hills of western Connecticut, Father Moriarity suggested we stop and visit Lauren Ford, the artist the two nuns had stayed with when they arrived from France. The movie *Come to the Stable*, written by Clare Boothe Luce, was based on this event and starred Elsa Lanchester in the role of the artist, Miss Amelia Potts, who was loosely patterned on Lauren Ford.

We turned into a dirt driveway with an arched gate and a sign that read "Sheepfold," and pulled in next to a low-lying red house, one of several small buildings, including a wooden tower of sorts, that all seemed to be stuck together.

Father Moriarity knocked on the rustic front door. A tall, gaunt woman with prominent front teeth, hair cut short in a bob just below her ears and bangs brushing her eyebrows opened the door holding a canary.

"Well, hello, Father. Who is this?" she asked, smiling.

"This is Tomie dePaola, Lauren. He's an art student who thinks he might want to be a Benedictine monk in Vermont. We are on our way to visit Reverend Mother Benedict," Father Moriarity told her.

"Hello, dearie," Lauren said. "How nice. Come in. This canary wasn't feeling too well, so I was giving him a cuddle. I'll just put him back in his cage, and then would you like to see my studio?"

I followed Lauren down a long sunlit hall, past a curtained alcove and into her bedroom-studio-aviary. A spindle bed surrounded by curtains made of a rich blue material occupied one corner. Her drawing board, with small tables filled with brushes and paints next to it, stood in a place to catch the best light. And there were cages and cages of canaries.

"I raise 'em," Lauren said. "They make good company. Being an artist can be a lonely profession, don't you find?"

I nodded yes, but my attention was caught by a beautiful half-finished painting of the Virgin and Child sitting in a Connecticut barn overlooking the Connecticut hills. I had never thought of depicting the Nativity in a familiar, contemporary setting.

"That's a new Christmas card I'm doing for the Artists' Guild," Lauren told me.

We went back to the sitting room, where a huge studio window looked out on fields dotted with Lauren's sheep. (Now I understood why it was called "Sheepfold.") Sheep and canaries!

Lauren and Father Moriarity were catching up on news when Lauren's friend and companion, Fanny Delehanty, joined us. She had a bob and bangs like Lauren, only Fanny's hair was silvery, and she was as round and short as Lauren was angular and tall. She was an artist too.

"Did Lauren show you our chapel?" Fanny asked. She took me down the hall to the alcove. Behind the curtain was an intimate space with a small altar against the back wall and several chairs on either side. "Mother Benedict and Mother Mary Aline said their prayers here," Fanny told me.

In the distance we heard a bell ringing. Lauren called down the hall, "That's the end of noon prayers, Tomie. Reverend Mother Benedict will be waiting for you."

We went off, promising to say good-bye at the monastery, where we would all meet at Vespers later in the afternoon.

The monastery looked like a Connecticut building, painted barn red, with the monastic gate echoing the arch that framed Sheepfold.

We went to a small entrance, rang the bell and entered a tiny vestibule with a door to the left and two doors to the right. One of the doors had a window-sized opening, called a grille, with a white curtain across it.

"*Benedicite*," a singsong voice said, and someone pulled the curtain aside.

"*Deus*, Mother," Father Moriarity answered. "We are here for an appointment with Reverend Mother Benedict."

"Just a moment, Father," the nun said. She came back and told us that Reverend Mother would see us in the parlor in St. Anthony's.

As we entered the parlor, my heart was beating as much from excitement as from the unfamiliarity and mysteriousness of it all. On the opposite wall was another larger grille. A door opened and in walked Reverend Mother Benedict. She was tall and graceful and her Benedictine habit was unlike any I had seen. The white material around her face and neck was snowy white, soft linen, not the stiff, starched material the teaching sisters wore. Mother Benedict sat and smiled directly at me. "Don't let the grille frighten you," she said. "It is meant to keep the public out, not the nuns in."

As Mother Benedict described a typical day (the nuns sang the

Divine Office, a combination of Psalms and prayers, seven times a day), I was quite taken with the beauty of it all. However, Mother Benedict knew that I was still at school and she gently insisted that I finish my studies before deciding to enter the monastery. She told me that if I had a real vocation, it would wait.

"Meanwhile, anytime you are home from Pratt, you are always welcome to come for a visit, to pray with us and learn more about Benedictine life."

I heard a soft knock on the door. It opened and in came a short, round-faced, bespectacled, smiling nun.

"Mother Placid is our artist," Reverend Mother told me. "I thought it would be nice for you to meet her. We Benedictines are interested in and involved with art, especially the Liturgy. That is the name for the 'official worship' of the Roman Catholic Church," she told me.

Mother Placid and I hit it off immediately. Within minutes we were laughing, telling each other art stories and promising to see each other again when I was home from Pratt.

During the next year, I visited Regina Laudis as much as I could. I once spent four days there and was thrilled to be allowed behind the grille to share some art techniques with Mother Placid in her studio. We had become best friends.

That summer, between my junior and senior year at Pratt, I attended an art school in Maine where I studied "true fresco," the old technique that was used by Fra Angelico and Giotto to decorate the walls of churches. So, before I headed off to Brooklyn for school, I had lots to share with Mother Placid and Lauren.

Then, just before I went home from Pratt for Christmas, I had a note from Reverend Mother Benedict inviting me to attend the Christmas Vigil, the two-hour chanting and singing of the Psalms and Lessons that takes place before the Midnight Mass. Flossie wasn't happy for me to miss Christmas Eve at home, but I heard my father say, "Aw, let him go if he wants to."

So off I went in the family Cadillac all the way to Bethlehem, driving under a cold, clear night sky with stars as big as silver dollars overhead. As I drove along, I fantasized that I was a shepherd following the Angel's instructions—"Go to the city of Bethlehem . . ."

When I arrived at Regina Laudis, I went to the chapel. Lauren and Fanny motioned me to come and sit next to them. "Come down to Sheepfold after the Mass," Fanny whispered to me. "We're having coffee, hot chocolate and hot sweet rolls."

The two extern sisters, Sister Prisca and Sister Maria Joseph,

entered and lit some candles at the curtained grille. The bell rang, and we could hear the nuns entering the choir behind the grille, which only added to the mystique.

The Vigil began: soloists singing Lessons; the *Schola*, a small group, singing in unison; then the choir of nuns chanting, first one side, then the other, answering back and forth, in perfect Gregorian Chant.

I was mesmerized. *Why don't they do this in parish churches?* I thought. *Because no one would come and sit for two hours before the hour-long Midnight Mass even began,* I realized.

After a short break, the bells began ringing again. The curtain behind the grille was opened by two white-veiled novices and the community filed in two by two, led by Reverend Mother Benedict. The candles on the altar were lit and flowers were brought in and

placed around the sanctuary. The priest came in wearing a vestment, hand-woven by the nuns, followed by the server, a farmer from nearby, dressed in a white robe with a hood and a silken cord around his waist, and two little boys, dressed the same way.

The Gregorian Chant for the Midnight Mass is among the most beautiful and sacred music ever composed. *"Hodie, Christus natus est . . . Today, Christ is born . . . "*

After Mass, Sister Prisca beckoned to me. She had a note from Reverend Mother Benedict and a hand-painted card from Mother Placid. I wished I could say "Merry Christmas" to them, but I knew that the "Grand Silence" was being observed.

I drove down to Sheepfold to join Lauren and Fanny and their friends. After delicious hot coffee and sweet rolls, we went out to one of the small barns where Lauren and Fanny had set up a small Nativity scene. In the dimly lit barn, we all sang, *"Hodie, Christus natus ..."*

I kissed everyone and drove the hour and a half home. When I got there, the outside Christmas lights were still on and Flossie was lying on the sofa.

"Did you have a nice time?" she asked.

"Oh yes," I answered.

"Good," Flossie said. "My goodness, it's four o'clock. Make your mother a drink and tell me all about it."

I made us both a drink and we talked. Finally I went upstairs to bed. As I lay down, all I could think about was how much I wanted to be a monk and to celebrate future Christmases in the Benedictine way.

A Weston Priory Christmas

In November of 1956, during the First Vespers of the Feast of Saint Gertrude, I became a novice at Weston Priory in Weston, Vermont, along with several other young men. I was given the name Placid, which was not only the name of my dear friend at Regina Laudis, but was a special name among Benedictines.

There is a charming story about Placid, one of Benedict's earliest monks. He was very young and had come to live at the monastery at Subiaco, Italy, along with another young man, Maur. One day Saint Benedict sent young Placid to the lake for water. Placid was so filled with obedience that he rushed into the lake and promptly floundered in the deep water. Saint Benedict had a vision of poor little Placid drowning and sent Maur to save him. Maur was also so obedient that he ran clear across the surface of the lake and plucked Placid to safety. (No wonder he became Saint Maur.)

So there I was, twenty-two years old, wearing the black tunic and short scapular of a Benedictine novice ready to celebrate his first season of Advent in its full liturgical starkness and beauty.

Life at Weston Priory in the fifties was primitive at best. I lived with the eight or nine novices on the second floor of a made-over chicken coop where the only heat came from a fireplace and a smoky stove on the first floor. Like many farmhouses of that era, several grates had been installed in the floor of the second story so that heat *might* rise and send up some warmth to our dormitory room filled with army surplus beds.

The simple accommodations were like being at Boy Scout camp except that in the monastery, the "Grand Silence" was observed from the end of "Compline," around eight in the evening, until "Prime," sung at about eight the next morning. In a contemplative monastery, all unnecessary talking was discouraged. But no matter how big or small, any talking during the Grand Silence was considered a breach of the "Rule." Yes, it was hard, especially for a chatterbox like me, but I did pretty well.

As the first Sunday of Advent approached, the prior, Father Bede, summoned me to his room. Brother Basil, who had returned from studies at a monastery in Canada, was already there.

Father Bede wanted our help in making the wreaths that would adorn the chapel during Advent. An enormous wreath would hang over the choir in our tiny chapel. One candle would be lit every night during the first week of Advent; two during the second week; and so on until four candles would be lit every evening at Vespers and during the Mass, or Eucharist, as we called it.

Brother Basil and I would also gather greens to make seven smaller wreaths. They would surround art I would create depicting the seven "O" antiphons that are sung during the last week of Advent vespers. The chapel, which had once been a small barn, had a pointed roof and ceiling with dark wooden beams and white plaster walls. We would hang one wreath at a time, starting where the walls met the lowest pitch of the roof, adding one each night on alternating sides until *O Emmanuel,* a depiction of the Christ Child in a white robe, was hung at the peak. (It was gratifying for this young novice to see how my fellow monks were moved by the greens and the colors that filled the simple little chapel every night.)

Father Bede had also learned that I had made some crèche figures while I was at Pratt, out of wood, paint and fabric dipped in plaster of Paris. They were very simple. He asked me to make figures of Our Lady and the Christ Child also for the chapel. Since obedience was the sterling monastic virtue, I said I would try.

"Good," Father Bede said. "The little shed attached to the chicken coop (the real one, not the old one where we slept) is warm from the chickens and no one will see you making it. Brother Basil will help. It will be a surprise." (Indeed, we managed to make the figures without anyone seeing them until Christmas Eve.)

I was pleased to play a part in making the Priory's celebration of Christmas so special, but a personal event happened that was amazing and lovely for me.

In my pre-retreat conference with Father Bede, where we had seven days of talks, silence and separation from the rest of the community before we were "clothed" as novices, Father Bede had told me of his dream to have bells that, when rung, would sound all the way down the valley to the village of Weston. All we had was a small, tinny-sounding bell fastened to a support outside the front door of the farmhouse, the main building of the Priory. Bells are important at a monastery. They toll day and night signaling the time for prayers, meals, meetings and other routines in monastic life.

When we began our retreat, Father Bede had told all of the candidates for the novitiate that we should pray for more vocations to join the Order. God would surely hear us at this special time in our lives. I had looked around silently. There were five of us. I'd let the others pray for vocations. I would pray for bells for Father Bede.

A few days after the ceremony of clothing and naming to become a novice, I was sent to Rutland with Brother Basil on an errand to the printer for the monastery. On the way, I told him that I had prayed for bells for Father Bede.

Brother Basil was shocked. "You don't pray for things like that," he scolded.

Too late. I already had. I guess I had squandered all that "close to God time" for some little bells. But it was Father Bede whom I genuinely loved and I wanted to make his wish come true.

It was several days before Christmas and outside it was snowing heavily. Breakfast was over, having been eaten in silence like all our meals. We were in the kitchen washing our breakfast dishes when someone knocked on the kitchen door. It was the driver of a truck parked in the driveway.

"Is there a Father 'Beady' here? I've got some bells for him outside on my flatbed."

Okay? Enough said. Brother Basil was the only one who knew about my prayers. He kept looking at me strangely. (From that time on, he called me "God's Spoiled Brat" in private.)

But he must have told Father Bede too, because when I saw him later that morning, he gave me a big hug and the "kiss of peace" on each cheek—a very Benedictine thing. The three bells were immediately put up in a temporary location until a proper belfry could be built. (We learned that the bells were a gift from a Mr. Paul Frietag, a benefactor from New Jersey. He was always buying things at auctions, and when he saw the three bells from some old trains, he decided to buy them and send them to Father Bede at Weston Priory.)

Finally it was Christmas Eve. The singing of the Christmas Vigil started at ten and finished at midnight in time for Midnight Mass. (There were three Masses at Christmas—midnight, dawn and mid-morning. And all of these had to be sung!) The monks entered the chapel to see my rustic statue of a young woman sitting next to a pine branch shaped to hold a wooden bowl filled with straw. Nestled in the straw was a Baby Jesus, looking like a little wrapped loaf of Italian bread. The vigil began. I sang the first Lesson, a solo, just like the days of the high school Christmas Sing—*"Consolamini, Consolamini, populus meus*—Be comforted, Be comforted my people . . ."

The chapel began to fill to overflowing with skiers who had come to Vermont for the Christmas holidays. Then the Mass at midnight began.

After Mass, the brothers gathered for hot chocolate and sticky buns in the refectory. It was all in silence except for the hugs and the kiss of peace. We read the notes and cards from the brothers to each other before stumbling off to our "chicken coop" to sleep for the few hours before dawn.

I couldn't sleep, so I put on my cloak and went outside. The night was dark and clear, yet so bright with stars that the snow looked that vivid blue we often have here in New England. It was like the year before at Regina Laudis. As I stood there, I heard the crystal-clear sounds of Father Bede's bells cutting through the cold air of the Vermont night.

A Vermont Farmhouse Christmas

CHRISTMAS 1957 FOUND ME BACK IN VERMONT, but not at Weston Priory. I had left the monastery at the end of January and moved to a small, primitive farmhouse in the village of Weston with my good friend Jack Schanhaar, the former Brother Basil. We were going to try an "experiment"—living simply as Benedictine Oblates, laypeople who use the *Rule of St. Benedict* as a guide for life.

We stayed closely connected to the Priory. The cook, Brother Gabriel, kept us supplied with fresh eggs from the "lay sisters," as Father Bede called the hens. Brother Martin instructed me in making whole-grain Anadama bread, and I got quite good at it. (I still make bread and nothing is as much fun as throwing dough around, knowing that in a little while the smell of fresh-baked bread is as good as it gets.)

Jack and I worked at the Priory. I was involved in launching a silk-screened Christmas card line, and Jack helped run the weaving workshop with one or two of the monks. We attended Mass every morning at five and Vespers in the late afternoon. We said the Psalms in English together in a small room we made into an "oratory," inspired by the chapel at Sheepfold. It was an unself-conscious,

59

simple existence, following the rhythms of the seasons, enjoying each other's company and making friends with wonderful people in the village.

I helped out at the Weston Playhouse, the local summer theater, painting scenery and eventually appearing onstage as well. Jack ended up teaching English at a private high school "downriver." We lived in Weston for over four years.

As Advent approached in December, we began to plan. Jack and I wanted to celebrate Advent and have a post–Midnight Mass "coffee, hot chocolate and hot sweet rolls," imitating Lauren Ford's get-together, in our farmhouse, beautifully decorated, with good friends around.

We went into the woods and once again gathered greens to make wreaths to hang on the front door, the plaster living room walls and for a large Advent wreath to hang over the dining room table that came with the house. Closer to Christmas we found a pretty good-shaped tree for our Christmas tree.

I made the batter for a Christmas plum pudding and passed it around to the few friends we'd invited for dinner on the Saturday night before the First Sunday of Advent. One of the Psalms begins, "Stir up, O Lord . . . " Well, on Saturday night, everyone got to "stir up" the plum pudding batter. The pudding was cooked and dowsed with booze, especially brandy, and put in a covered tin. Then, at Christmas dinner, à la Mrs. Cratchit, the freshly steamed plum pudding complete with flaming brandy would be brought to the table.

As the days passed, we topped up the brandy as needed. I admit I was concerned about the way the pudding was soaking up the booze.

It was bound to explode when the warm brandy was poured over it and it was lit! (It didn't, but the flames certainly lit up the room!)

I made Nativity figures of Mary, Joseph, Baby Jesus and a flying angel out of Coke bottles, plaster of Paris and cloth soaked in the plaster, all painted and "antiqued," silently thanking Lauren for her inspiration.

But we were as poor as the proverbial church mice or ex-monks (in our case). What to do about decorations? There was always popcorn, cranberry garlands or paper chains, but that all screamed of "kindergarten."

I was reading all kinds of books about Christmas traditions when I came across an essay about the ancient custom of bringing greens into the house or hall for the winter solstice and how this custom was resurrected during the early medieval period. A fir tree was brought into the great hall along with the Yule log, big enough to burn for the thirteen or so days between Christmas and Epiphany, January 6. The tree hung on a wall upside down. It was wrapped with crisscrossed ribbons and decorated with gilded apples and roses. It was called a "Mary Tree."

At the same time, in one of the women's magazines, I found a craft page on how to make artificial roses from tissue paper. I would make my own version of a "Mary Tree."

A good friend from art school responded to a letter from me by sending packets and packets of brightly colored tissue—hot pink, orange, red, turquoise, lavender—all the colors of the rainbow and more. I got to work. They were fairly easy to make and, in a short time, I had a good-sized box filled with the brightly colored roses.

I only lost a few to my charming Siamese cat, Tica, short for Scholastica. She enjoyed her roses as well, carrying them around in her teeth, hiding them in secret places and bringing them out when she wanted to show off. (It was a plan that worked. Tica never touched the roses on the tree.)

Jack and I decided to forgo the gilded apples. Real gold leaf was out of the question. Gold paint would look terrible on crabapples, already shriveling by Christmas. Macs would be too heavy. Artificial apples were out of the budget, as well as Christmas tree lights. So it was roses only!

It was a beautiful tree and everyone who came to visit was full of admiring compliments.

That was in 1957. Except for a few Christmases when I have been traveling (I can actually count those on both hands), I have always had a Christmas tree covered in, by now, the tenth or eleventh generation of paper roses. Now there are tiny white lights and folk art ornaments, painted Mexican tin, white birds and other things I've picked up along the way, hanging amongst the roses. But they are the focal point.

I toyed with the idea of real roses in glass vials once, but when I held some real roses against my tissue paper ones, they paled. What a surprise! But maybe not—maybe at Christmastime, art or artifice can masquerade quite successfully as life. I guess it's really a Christmas sort of thing.

A San Francisco Christmas

W HEN I MOVED TO SAN FRANCISCO IN 1967, one of the things that I loaded into my VW bus was a bag of paper roses for my Christmas tree.

I was moving west to get my master's degree. My dream of writing and illustrating books for children had come true when *The Wonderful Dragon of Timlin* was published the year before, and I knew I would continue creating children's books. But, since 1962, I had been making a living teaching art at the college level, and a master's of fine arts would boost me up the professional ladder. As a full professor, I would receive the monetary benefits that went with it, which would give me more time to concentrate on my art.

I found a great place to live. It was a typical three-story "flat" building constructed shortly after the Great Earthquake in 1906. In San Francisco, the difference between a "flat" and an "apartment" is that an apartment building has one entrance with a shared lobby whereas a flat building has a separate street entrance for each unit.

My flat was up a long flight of stairs to the third floor. To enter,

I pulled a metal contraption on the wall, which opened the front door into a wide hall. All the rooms were off of it, and every room had windows, so the flat was filled with light.

I had a living room with a working fireplace, a dining room, a butler's pantry, a kitchen, a utility room off the kitchen, a bathroom, lots of closets and two bedrooms, one in the front and the second, which was the larger one, in the back looking west. I chose that bedroom for my studio. From it I saw spectacular sunsets, and in the summer, I watched the fog roll in from the ocean. All of this for under two hundred dollars a month.

The location was great too. I was one block from the top of Nob Hill and two blocks from the California Street cable car line that went directly to the center of the downtown area. I could walk to Fisherman's Wharf and North Beach, the Italian neighborhood and the home of Big Al's, with the dubious honor of being the first topless joint in San Francisco.

I paid for electricity, gas, telephone, and trash removal. San Francisco did not have free trash collection in those days. The company that serviced our neighborhood called itself—would you believe it—"The Scavengers."

My first Christmas was hard to get used to—no snow, leaves on the trees and flowers in window boxes. But Christmas decorations were in abundance. If the flats or apartments had bay windows (a popular feature in San Francisco), blinking Christmas trees looked out at everyone on the streets and passersby looked back. Many residents put up their trees on Thanksgiving and they were gone the day after Christmas. I've always waited until just before Christmas to put my tree up and traditionally leave it up until at least January 6—the Feast of the Epiphany (or the Three Kings).

Christmas tree lots sprung up overnight. My good friend Mary Jo, who had been an art student of mine, had moved to San Francisco several months after I did. She lived in the neighborhood, so we went Christmas tree shopping together in my VW bus. I took the two back seats out and stowed them inside my front door. We drove around, looking for not only the best bargains, but also the best-shaped trees. All the trees already had crossed wooded bases. I guess if you wanted to use a tree stand that you could fill with water, they'd remove the wooden bases, but hey—it sure made it easier to set up the tree.

We found a lot on Union Street run by two Italian brothers. They gave us a good price, and the trees looked fresh. Mary Jo picked a small tree. I chose a long-needle pine because they don't shed as quickly as a fir.

When Christmastime was over, I had to pay extra for "The Scavengers" to take away my tree. I wasn't about to break the law and just leave the poor thing on the corner after dark. Of course, lots of "criminals" did and Christmas trees piled up on corners, then miraculously disappeared overnight.

By the next Christmas, I had a really nice circle of friends, so I decided to resurrect my tradition of a post-Christmas party. Everyone has parties before Christmas. I always enjoy having my party after Christmas. I like to keep Christmas going as long as I can.

My party would be on Saturday, December 28. I sent out the invitations, got a great response and sat down to plan the decorations. All my friends were into decorating. I was an artist. I had to "compete."

My tree would have white lights, my paper roses and baker's clay hearts. I'd put roping of pine branches over the doorways with bright red bows in the corners. I'd do the New England thing of white electric candles in the windows and of course I'd have lots of votive candles in clear and red glasses scattered around the flat.

Mary Jo and I went back to the Union Street tree lot to get our trees. I had stopped off earlier to give them measurements for my roping. As we were picking out our trees, I noticed that they had a lot of little trees between two and three feet, all with bases.

"Hey, *Paesano*," I said to one of the brothers. "Do you think you'll have any of those little trees left over?"

"I dunno, maybe yes, maybe no," he answered.

"Oh yeah?" the other brother said. "I told him not to buy so many little trees. We're gonna have lots left over. Why, you want 'em?"

"Maybe," I said, not wanting to look or sound too interested. "I'm having a party after Christmas. Maybe a few little trees would look nice as decorations."

The brothers turned their backs and talked to each other.

"Tell you what. We gotta close down the lot by six o'clock Christmas Eve. Come by after one o'clock and we'll see what we can do." We shook hands on it.

On the afternoon of Christmas Eve, I took the seats out of the bus again and picked up Mary Jo. When we got to the lot, it was not busy, but it was pretty picked over. A few last-minute bargain hunters were wandering around hoping to get a better price. I had the distinct feeling that the brothers were nobody's fools. No one was getting a bargain that day—except me.

The older brother motioned me over. "How many do you want?" he asked.

"How much each?" I asked.

The younger brother came over. "We got eighty! I'll let you have all eighty for seventy-five dollars!"

"Deal," I said.

It took three trips and I recruited some neighborhood kids to carry the trees up to the flat. It became a neighborhood event as more and more kids joined in.

Fortunately, because of the moist evenings in San Francisco, the trees were still pretty fresh. They came in a variety of heights, and what a delicious smell! Mary Jo helped me place them along the walls of the dining room and in groups in the broad hallway. They looked sensational.

Saturday came and I had all the electric candles burning in the windows, the Christmas tree glowing brightly, the votives giving off their soft light from all the corners of the flat and little undecorated trees everywhere. Tomie's forest. I had done it!

The evening was a great success and the eighty trees were the "talk of the party." I certainly was the Decorating Divo. I knew some of my guests would steal the idea for next year, but by then it would be "old news," and I had a whole year to come up with a fantastic idea for next year's post-Christmas party.

Then the party was over and it dawned on me that I had a more immediate conundrum. How do I get rid of all these trees? Aha. "The Scavengers." Maybe they were "Paesanos" too!

On Monday morning I kept my eyes open for their truck and when I saw it coming up the hill, I ran down the back stairs to where the trash barrels were kept and did some fast talking to the three "Scavengers." The Boss followed me upstairs to look over the situation.

"A piece of cake," he said, and proceeded to toss the trees out the back windows. The guys below grabbed them and threw them into the bed of the truck, which promptly chewed them up. "Fifty bucks," the Boss said. I handed him the money and some extra for the "guys."

I kept the big tree up longer. I briefly entertained the thought of leaving it on the corner after dark, but I didn't want to tempt fate.

As for next year's party, maybe I could get a really good price on amaryllis. They'd look great in groups all over the flat.

They did!

A New York Christmas

As CHRISTMAS 1983 APPROACHED, I was between houses in New London, New Hampshire, and neither my longtime assistant and friend, Bob, nor I was enthusiastic about decorating the house I was renting temporarily. Our friend Charles had invited us to his Christmas party in New York. After that he was going south to spend Christmas with his family, and he offered his apartment to Bob and me while he was away. I hadn't been in the Big Apple for Christmas in years and Bob never had. We accepted with pleasure.

Charles's apartment, though small, was comfortable and inviting and warmly decorated with folk art objects. (Charles and I both share a mania for folk art.) I knew he would have a fabulous tree and he did, filled with cloth-quilted hearts he had made and dried flowers stuck among the branches. The Christmas party was great and went late into the night. His guests were mostly theater people, so the conversation was lively and full of gossip.

The next day Charles took us to the ultimate Christmas event, the Christmas stage show at Radio City Music Hall. Watching the Rockettes perform their wooden soldier routine makes it so easy to

be a kid again. But the final "act" was over-the-top wonderful—a Nativity scene with angels flying around and a procession complete with live sheep, donkeys and camels.

One of the dancers was a friend of Charles's, so when the show was over, we got a "personal" backstage tour complete with a peek at the "zoo" in the basement under the huge stage. For an old tap dancer like me, it was a thrill to see the dressing rooms, the backstage area and the hydraulic mechanism that moved the sections of the stage up and down. I stood center stage, looked out into the "house" and did a quick little "time step." (*Finally,* I thought, *I'm onstage at Radio City Music Hall.*)

Before we left, we got a quick peek at the art deco rest rooms. The "Powder Rooms" for ladies were fantastic—murals decorated the walls and long rows of vanity tables with round mirrors lined the walls under them. Supposedly, Georgia O'Keefe did one of the murals, but I couldn't tell which one it might be.

We went out into the cold night and walked to Rockefeller Center to see the tree before heading uptown to Charles's cozy apartment.

Charles left the next morning, and Bob and I played "pretend New Yorkers" for the next few days. The city is at its best at Christmas and we had a great time exploring our Upper West Side neighborhood, window-shopping, looking at all the Christmas decorations and department store windows along Fifth and Madison Avenues. The smell of roasting chestnuts filled the air as last-minute shoppers and merrymakers just having a good time crowded the sidewalks. We loved being among them.

Christmas Eve was freezing! The temperature had fallen below zero and a wind off both rivers put Manhattan into a deep freeze. I had coerced Bob, a good Lutheran, to join me for Midnight Mass at the Paulist church next to Lincoln Center. The neighborhood had a good-sized Hispanic population, which I hadn't known. So there was a wonderful flavor to the Mass with mariachis playing and a *posadas* procession of children dressed as Mary and Joseph and the shepherds looking for a place to stay. At the end of the Mass, the tiny actors filed out and became a living Nativity before the altar in the sanctuary. Well, Radio City Music Hall had met its match!

The next day, Christmas Day, we walked downtown through Central Park to the Plaza Hotel for a four o'clock dinner in their famous Oak Room. I had made the reservation weeks and weeks before. Bob and I got there early so I could have one of their famous martinis in the (at that time) "Men Only" Oak Bar.

When it was time for our reservation, we were ushered into the high-ceilinged, dark oak wood-paneled room, colorful murals looking down at us. Our table for two was nestled up against a curved banquette. On a table next to us was a phone. "We should have someone call us," I whispered to Bob. Menus that hid us from sight were "proffered" to us. (Don't you love that word? At other restaurants they "hand" you the menu. At the Plaza they "proffer." I have been to many restaurants, but no one did it like the Plaza.)

I don't remember much about the dinner and the wine except that it was festive, delicious, expensive and a wonderful way to have Christmas dinner.

What I do remember is the table near us. It was a large round one filled with a multigenerational family, all dressed to the "nines." An older woman with white hair coiffed within an inch of its life, tastefully bejeweled in diamonds and equally tastefully dressed in black, was obviously in charge. There was only one child—a little girl about seven years old, dressed in gauzy pink ruffles, pink ruffled socks and black patent-leather Mary Janes. Her beauty-parlored curly hair was topped with a big pink bow. She seemed well behaved and bored out of her mind. No one was talking to her, but she had a look on her face that said, "I've been in this situation before."

The waiter started taking dessert orders. When he came to the little girl, he said, "And little miss, for you we have a very special dessert, our Santa ice cream." I tried not to stare, but I was fascinated. I really wanted to see how this was all going to turn out.

Finally a brigade of servers arrived with trays filled with fancy desserts. The waiter himself took the little girl's special dessert, placed it in front of her and stepped back. It was a pink and white fruit-ice Santa Claus standing amongst globes of strawberry and vanilla ice cream. She stared at it. Everyone looked lovingly at her. The older woman said, "Isn't that lovely, dear? A Santa Popsicle!"

The little girl picked up the Santa and promptly bit off his head. The rest of the table froze in absolute silence.

"Oh, well," I said to Bob. "This *is* the Plaza, after all. 'Eloise' is alive and well."

A Santa Fe Christmas

AFTER MY 1991 CHRISTMAS PARTY, I DECIDED THAT ENOUGH WAS ENOUGH. The party had grown and grown. I had invited many of my neighbors, and it seemed as if they all brought friends. Suddenly I found myself running out of food, space and familiar faces. But there was a dilemma! How do I have a party and not invite all the people I had been inviting for years? Bob, my assistant, gave me a solution. Go away for Christmas!

It was decided. I would leave New London for the next two Christmases. Bob would get a rest from decorating the multiple trees, and after two years, everyone would be used to no party. I could begin again—if I dared.

It didn't take me five minutes to decide where I would spend the Christmas of 1992. I had fallen in love with Santa Fe, its wonderful restaurants, galleries, museums and folk art shops. I had made some endearing friendships in my visits there—especially Alice Ann Biggerstaff. We had met in Kansas City, Missouri, when Alice Ann was a head designer at Hallmark Cards. She had retired to Santa Fe, and I had visited her on my first trip to the "City Different." Alice Ann had become my tour guide, sharing her love, knowledge and friends. I have rarely felt quite so welcome in a place, and I was assured of a busy "social whirl" during my visit.

I made early reservations at the then-funky La Posada de Santa Fe. (It is now pretty fancy.) It was within easy walking distance of the Plaza, galleries, shops, restaurants and bars. Alice Ann sent me tons of information and newspapers filled with all the holiday events scheduled. The Christmas party invitations started to come in too!

I flew to Albuquerque, rented a car and headed for Santa Fe. I could see snow on the Sangre de Cristo Mountains along the way, and when I drove into Santa Fe, a light snow was falling. I got out of the car at La Posada, and immediately smelled the Piñion smoke from all the kiva fireplaces in the city.

Of course, church bells were ringing. I checked into my *casita*—a more or less freestanding "little house"—and called Alice Ann. We would meet for drinks at the bar, go to El Farol on Canyon Road for *tapas* and end up at Vanessie's piano bar. It sounded like a good way to spend my first Friday night.

Santa Fe was all decked out for Christmas. *Farolitos*—the Mexican tradition of small candles placed in paper bags to "light the way"—lined the parapets of the buildings. (Now the lights were electric, but the glowing effect was startling nevertheless.)

In New England, pine roping and wreaths are traditional during the Christmas season. In Santa Fe, evergreens complemented with *ristras*, circles and swags of dried red chiles hanging down, and *Flores de Nochebuena*, more commonly known as poinsettias, were everywhere.

Alice Ann and I had a great night. We made plans to drive to Chimayo, a small Hispanic village north of Santa Fe, the next day. Chimayo is a weaving center famous for its "miraculous" *sanctuario*— a beautiful old adobe chapel; its equally "miraculous" dried *chiles* (it is believed *El Niño*—the Christ Child himself—waters the peppers); and a fabulous restaurant, Rancho de Chimayo, where we had a long lunch of *enchiladas* and *margaritas*. On the way back to my hotel, Alice Ann advised me to rest up, because in the late afternoon of the next day, we were going to the Plaza for *Las Posadas*. I did as I was told, and I was glad, because I was in for a treat.

We met in the Plaza along with what seemed like the whole of Santa Fe. The center of the Plaza was stunning from colored lights glowing in the trees and real *farolitos* lining the paths.

Alice Ann was explaining that *Las Posadas* was the search for a place where the Child could be born, when a hush came over the crowd. A young couple dressed as Mary and Joseph (quite often they are a brother and sister) entered and began their walk around the Plaza, followed by musicians singing old songs in Spanish. Suddenly a devil appeared on a balcony over a storefront and yelled, "No room." The crowd booed. Alice and I joined in. This went on and on, the boos getting louder and louder, as the devil rushed from balcony to balcony, yelling at them. (Actually they needed two devils because the Plaza is so large.)

Finally, the gates at the Palace of the Governors opened up, and Mary and Joseph went in. Now they were safe and everyone relaxed. A bonfire burned in the courtyard, and hot chocolate and *bizcochitos*— special cookies—were served. The crowd was full of the Christmas spirit, and Christmas was still several days away.

78

The few days and nights before Christmas Eve were filled with forays to museums around town, shopping for folk art, lunch at The Shed (the waitress had to bring me a glass of milk when she saw that I was about to explode from the hot chiles in my enchilada) and evening parties in homes decorated in a distinct Santa Fe style. Even my *casita* looked festive with an enormous *Flor de Nochebuena* from Bob, in lieu of a Christmas tree.

At dusk on Christmas Eve, Alice Ann and I joined some of her friends for the "Christmas Eve Walk" up Canyon Road, the ever-present Piñion wood smoke in the air. Group after group carrying candles and singing carols followed the narrow winding street of galleries, restaurants, bars and private homes all decorated with genuine *farolitos*. (Electric ones were not permitted.) *Luminarios,* or bonfires, blazed along the way. My favorite sight, though, was a festive group carrying a Menorah made out of flashlights duct-taped together, singing a Hanukah song. After some hot coffee and a bite to eat, Alice Ann and I headed off in her Jeep Cherokee for Midnight Mass in Santa Domingo Pueblo. The small adobe church in the village was decorated with blinking lights, and a remarkable radiating star on the Christmas tree rivaled any Times Square sign. There were no chairs, so people stood or sat on the floor, the crowd dotted with the brightly colored shawls worn by many of the older women.

A young Franciscan priest began the Mass with drums and flutes playing. When he intoned *Gloria in Excelsis Deo,* the sound of hundreds of birds chirping up in the choir loft was made by young boys with "water whistles." It was a heart-stopping moment.

After Mass, we visited Orlinda, an ancient Native American

woman from the pueblo whom Alice Ann had befriended years ago. It had become a tradition to stop by her house for something to eat.

Mass over, our bellies full, it was after two in the morning when we headed back to Santa Fe. As we drove on the highway, we noticed in the headlights decorated artificial trees every so often standing in the median. They weren't there to commemorate highway accidents, like the crosses surrounded with artificial flowers; they were just there because the people of Santa Fe liked Christmas!

Well, I thought, *I'm certainly glad I came.*

I've been back to Santa Fe, but never for Christmas. I'm afraid that to try to repeat such a perfect celebration would be sheer folly. I'll live quite happily with all my memories.

A Whitebird Christmas

Well, it was time for me to spend Christmas again at Whitebird, the home where I still live in New Hampshire. Even though I wouldn't be hosting a huge post-Christmas party, I would have a houseful of guests, including two adorable Australian boys and their parents. My friends Jenny and Tony and their son, Fraser, who was also my godson, were living and working in New York City, where they had come from their home in Melbourne. Through them, I had met Sara and her son, Alexander, or Allie, and a teaching colleague of theirs, Paul. They were all excited to be coming to spend Christmas in a picture-perfect New England village instead of on a sunny Australian beach.

"Tomie," Tony asked, "will there be snow? I want my little boy to make a snow angel. I've never made one either. Are they easy to make?"

I assured Tony that snow angels were not that hard, and that I would do my personal "snow dance" to produce a "White Christmas."

Phone calls went back and forth between New London and New York. Federal Express would be delivering packages from "Santa" for the boys. "I'm worried that there won't be enough room in the rental car," Jenny said.

Sara was a good cook, so she and I discussed the Christmas Day menu. We'd have roast beef, Yorkshire pudding, roasted potatoes, some sort of vegetable and flaming plum pudding and mince pie for dessert.

I would provide Christmas trees—yes—trees, compliments of Bob, who would deck out the big tree in the living room with the "famous" paper roses, folk art ornaments and thousands of white lights. The dining room would have small trees with lights arranged around the room, shades of San Francisco. The boys would have trees in their bedrooms. Trees with tiny white lights would be seen glowing in the night through the large picture window that looked out on my meadow.

I ordered wreaths with red bows for all the doors, flowers for the rooms, holly, mistletoe and dozens of poinsettia plants. Paul called to make sure that the New Hampshire State Liquor Store had plenty of Stoli vodka.

Packages, packages and more packages arrived from Santa, and I found out that in Australia, Santa wraps all the presents he brings. When we were growing up at 26 Fairmount Avenue, Santa's gifts were under the tree unwrapped on Christmas morning.

Then, a few days before the guests arrived, snow started falling, lightly at first, then heavier and thicker. We would indeed have a "White Christmas."

The snow tapered off on the twenty-third so the travelers could drive north without incident. Hugs, kisses and the unloading of luggage and shopping bags full of *more* presents took a while.

Jenny commandeered a portion of "the bench"—kitchen counter

to us—to act as the boys' personal snack bar. Certain "rules" were laid out. No water from the door of the fridge without asking first; no screaming "Mama" when the mothers were as close as the next room; toys that had a million pieces had to be played with in the basement or their bedrooms; and only one rule for adults, no Stoli until the sun went down!

That night, the snow began again. Fraser and Allie pressed their faces against the windows. The next day would be just the day for making snow angels.

Everyone was busy from the time we woke up on Christmas Eve day. Tony took over "cut flowers and holly" duty. Sara helped me get some "prep" work done in the kitchen. Jenny had "feed the boys" duty. Paul was "man of all work," helping all of us. Bob worked outside with the snow thrower and shovels.

An inner courtyard separates the house from the studio I had designed and added to the original barn. When it snows, drifts roar down the metal roofs and into the courtyard below, creating a snowscape that might rival Antarctica (if I had some penguins). The enormous piles would be perfect for snow angels.

Tony put sweaters, coats, hats, scarves, earmuffs, mittens and boots on the boys, and after getting last-minute instructions, they went outside. We watched through a window as Fraser took off his mittens and touched the snow. A wail filled the courtyard. "I'm burning!" Fraser shouted, and ran inside. No one had told him that snow was cold.

Tony tried to get Allie to make a snow angel, but he wasn't about to lie down in that scary stuff. Allie went inside too. In desperation, Tony threw himself faceup on a snowbank, waved his arms back and forth, and got up. There it was. A perfect snow angel. Jenny rushed out to take a picture of it. Neither boy wanted anything to do with it.

We cheered Tony as he came in shivering and covered in snow. We immediately broke the Stoli rule.

Early in the evening, I put on Christmas music. We lit the Christmas tree and hung the stockings from the mantel before the boys headed off to bed to "wait for Santa." We poured glasses of Stoli and toasted the Aussies' first American Christmas. We laughed, reminisced, told stories, gossiped and decided to have our own "visions of sugarplums dancing in our heads."

As I turned out the lights, a fresh sprinkling of glittery snow began to fall. It would be as perfect a Whitebird Christmas as it could be, at home and with good friends.

Tomie dePaola is best known for his books for children. He has written and/or illustrated over 200 books.

Born in Meriden, Connecticut, in 1934, dePaola received his BFA from Pratt Institute in Brooklyn, New York, and his MFA from the California College of Arts in Oakland, California. He received a doctoral equivalency in fine arts from Lone Mountain College in San Francisco.

In addition to writing and illustrating children's books, dePaola taught for several years in art and theater departments in colleges in California, Massachusetts and New Hampshire. He has designed stage sets and greeting cards and painted church murals. He designed costumes and served as artistic director for the Children's Theatre Company of Minneapolis's productions of his books. His artwork has been exhibited in one-man shows throughout the world.

DePaola has received many prestigious awards, including the Smithson Medal from the Smithsonian Institution, the Kerlan Award from the University of Minnesota for his "singular attainment in children's literature," and the Regina Medal from the Catholic Library Association.

He was also the United States nominee in 1990 for the Hans Christian Andersen Award in illustration. The American Library Association named *Strega Nona* a Caldecott Honor Book and *26 Fairmount Avenue* a Newbery Honor Book.

The University of Connecticut, Georgetown University and Colby-Sawyer College, among others, have granted him honorary doctoral degrees. In 1999, he was selected for the New Hampshire Governor's Arts Award of Living Treasure.

DePaola makes his home in New London, New Hampshire, where he works in a renovated 200-year-old barn. *Christmas Remembered* is his first book *for all ages.*